Christian Meditation

Reviving a Lost Art

By

Mark Hollis

CONTENTS

CONTENTS

Introduction

I know enough about myself to understand that not everything in me is good. As the Bible puts it, "The human heart is the most deceitful of all things, and desperately wicked. Who really knows how bad it is?" (Jeremiah 17:9, New Living Translation). So, who would want to take the time to uncover the garbage that meditation can uncover? After all, ignorance is bliss.

Meditation as a secular discipline must be a depressing endeavor. Apart from salvation through Jesus Christ, there really is nothing good in us. I really do not understand why meditation is so popular among people who are not Christians. I guess the goal of meditation for a non-Christian consists of trying to think of something good and focusing all their energy on that one thing in order to feel better. For the person who does not know Jesus personally, meditation must be more about forgetting than an honest encounter with what lay inside the human heart and mind.

But there is one thing right from the start I want you to know about this book. It assumes that you have come to an awareness of your own sin and accepted the forgiveness of Jesus Christ. Though we are not perfect, we have accepted Jesus Christ as our personal Savior and his presence lives in us. "...Christ lives within you, so even though your body will die because of sin, the Spirit gives you life because you have been made right with God" (Romans 8:10, New Living Translation).

But what is the nature of the life of Jesus in me? Some conclude that Jesus lives in our spirit, but our body and mind remain more or less trapped in the grip of sin. I cannot buy into the idea that my body and mind are outside of the influence of the life of Jesus in me. My body has been touched by the supernatural power of Jesus several times. I have seen too many people testify to the physical result of Jesus the Healer when he makes himself known. I believe that the presence of Jesus in our life means redemption for our body as well as our spirit. It may not be automatic, or instantly complete, but our physical healing is most certainly present in some way with the presence of Jesus in us.

The same is so for the mind. We are introduced to a Jesus in the Bible who's presence resulted in people being restored to their "right mind" (Luke 8:35). The Bible encourages us, "Don't copy the behavior and customs of this world, but let God transform you into a new person by changing the way you think" (Romans 12:2, New Living Translation).

Our minds are constantly busy, which is not always a good thing. They are not always our friend when it comes to hearing the voice of God. By actively exercising our mind we can train our mind to better reflect the presence of Jesus in us. We can follow the instructions of the Apostle Paul to the Philippians (chapter 4 verse 8), "And now, dear brothers and sisters, one final thing. Fix your thoughts on what is true, and honorable, and right, and pure, and lovely, and admirable. Think about things that are excellent and worthy of praise."

Meditation, as described in this book, includes three general steps. First, is about becoming aware of the current state of our body and our mind. It puts us in touch with our weakness. Second, meditation prepares our body and mind to be a kind of "clean page" for God to write on. Third, it helps us realize the strength of Jesus in us. His strength forms in us new eyes to view our lives and the world.

Meditation will strengthen your walk with Jesus by helping you live convinced that Jesus is actively speaking to you and working to complete you as a whole person. The results of meditation will be very self-evident as you encounter life each day with the secure understanding that God's peace is inside no matter what. We will declare to God with the prophet Isaiah, "You will keep in perfect peace all who trust in you, all whose thoughts are fixed on you!" (Isaiah 26:3, New Living Translation).

CHAPTER 1

CHRISTIAN MEDITATION?

Teach me, LORD, the meaning of your laws,
and I will obey them at all times.
Explain your law to me, and I will obey it;
I will keep it with all my heart.
Psalm 119:33-34, TEV

Understanding God's Word is serious business. It is the duty of not only the clergy and scholars, but of every Christian believer. There are many ways to grow in our understanding of God's truth. The easiest way is to have someone else think and hear for us. We arrive once or twice a week at church to hear 45 minutes of someone else's explanation from a portion of the Bible. Perhaps the preacher has dug into the depths of God's Word and mined valuable insights through painstaking mental exercise. But what is likely closer to the truth is that the pastor has looked to yet someone else—a saint long past, a modern communicator, a popular author or a recent conference DVD—for his insights.

Don't misunderstand me, I am not saying the insights of others are useless or in any way inferior. I have been a preacher for more than 20 years. I have used the thoughts of others more often than I should have. What I am saying is that I too often opted for the ease and convenience of borrowing (stealing?) from others. I am now, however, becoming aware of my own proficiency at hearing and understanding without the aid of anyone else. I will be the first to admit, however, that it is not easy work. It is much easier to download a message and listen to how God talked with someone else than it is to put in the effort that leads to a unique personal encounter with God's voice. Book publishers and websites promoting sermon ideas and full-text messages are making millions of dollars. Conference DVD's sell like hotcakes when the material is good enough to preach to someone else. Could this be an indication that the time and effort needed to invest in a deep personal understanding of God's Word is a price some of us are unwilling to pay? Instant and reformatted messages may be well-suited to our busy lifestyles, but are we missing out on a valid and deep experience with a personal God who is speaking directly to us in order that He can speak through us? Are we declining the invitation to be prophet, and settling for messenger of a prophet's message?

Perhaps we are not as unwilling as we are unskilled. Nelson says, "Meditation is a lost art for many Christians, but the practice needs to be cultivated again." I agree. The discipline of meditation is almost unheard of in our churches. As I travel and preach I often lead the congregation in a meditation exercise that centers on the text of my message. If the congregation allows me to lead them, and they apply themselves to the exercise, the results are incredible. Often someone will come up to me after the service and tell me that my message was good, but the message that God revealed to them during the meditation exercise was life-changing!

At the heart of the issue for me is the belief that God is speaking to each one of us. True, He sometimes speaks to us through other individuals, books, DVD's or even (occasionally) the internet. But primarily God wants us to hear His voice directly. "The LORD would speak with Moses face-to-face, just as a man speaks with a friend. Then Moses would return to the camp. But the young man who was his helper, Joshua son of Nun, stayed in the Tent" (Exodus 33:10-11 TEV, emphasis mine). Moses received the experience of a face-to-face encounter with God, who spoke to him as a friend. Aaron stayed behind in the tent waiting for Moses to communicate what he and God had talked about. The people in turn waited for Aaron to tell them what Moses had said about his conversation with God on the mountain. The farther we get from a first hand dialog with God, the harder it is to know him as a friend. In fact, I am of the opinion that unless we cultivate a first-hand dialog with God, we cannot truly know him as friend.

My hope is that you have a desire to gain an understanding of God's truth through first-hand experience. I am not talking about an exercise in cultivating your prophetic gift or how to receive a word of knowledge or other miraculous insight reserved for super-saints. I am talking about training your mind to focus intently on God and His word. No doubt God has incredible things He wants you to hear and understand. If you are to hear them, you must take the time to learn to listen and to understand. Or else you will be forced to spend a lot of money to attend another conference...

I am talking about the process of what is commonly called "meditation". Now before you close this book and judge me as a New Age peddler of psycho-theology, let me say that the Bible is not unaware of or averse to the discipline of meditation. It is a process that aided the Psalmist is his understanding of God's truth. The Psalms open with a description of one who is blessed, saying that "in His law he meditates day and night" (Psalm 1:2b). The late hours of the night are often referred to as ideal times for meditation, "My eyes anticipate the night watches, that I may meditate on Thy word" (Ps 119:148, see also Ps 4:4; 63:6).

In the New Testament, Apostle Paul advises his younger companion, Timothy, with regard to meditation. Paul exhorts Timothy to give himself to the task of reading the Scripture in public, as well as preaching and teaching its truth. The process that was to prepare him for this important task was to "...meditate on these things; give yourself entirely to them," (1Tim 4:13-15). The NASB translation of this verse gives an indication of the personal effort required by Timothy. He is to "...take pains with these things; be absorbed in them..." (1Tim 4:15).

The Bible views meditation as an effective discipline which aids a person in understanding God's truth. It is different from receiving a word of prophecy or any of the other spiritual gifts dealing with knowledge and understanding. The spiritual gifts are a work of the Spirit's initiative. Meditation is an exercise resulting from the initiative of the individual.

Meditation has become unpopular among Christians for at least two main reasons. The first is its identity with other religions. For the Buddhist, meditation is the means by which the reality of all things is to be learned. It is the means of salvation as it provides the understanding necessary for liberation from the cycle of pain and suffering including rebirth, sickness, old age and death. For the Buddhist, there is no personal god who has acted as creator and maintainer of the universe. There is only the individual who must become aware of the truth of suffering and the impermanent nature of all things. Through the effort of meditation one is able to realize the insight to be liberated and put an end to all suffering.

Likewise Hinduism has taught the effectiveness of meditation for gaining special spiritual powers. Through the discipline of meditation one can effectively manipulate the gods and control the circumstances in and around their life. Mind reading, soul traveling, out-of-body experiences and a host of other mental abilities have become associated with the Eastern concept of meditation. As a result, when someone mentions "meditation", images of chanting Buddhist monks and wild-eyed yogis come to mind. This is an unwarranted response. Meditation is a skill that may be used by Christianity as well as other religions. In this respect meditation is much like the discipline of prayer, which is used by all religious philosophies.

The second reason for the unpopularity of meditation among Christians is the nature of meditation itself. It is plain hard work. Eliminating distraction, becoming aware of your own mind's activities, focusing on a subject and cultivating mindfulness are difficult mental exercises. They are strenuous and demand a certain amount of discipline. In the same way physical exercise benefits the body, meditation produces health for your mind that enables it to perform at a higher level of efficiency.

The association of meditation with other religions has resulted in a profound scepticism. Many keep the idea of meditation at arm's length for fear that spiritual harm will result if it is practiced. Most Eastern religious philosophies prioritize meditation as a means by which the mind is emptied and kept empty. The goal for the meditator is to keep thoughts (both good and bad) from taking root in the mind. Through this discipline a sense of freedom can be attained.

What an empty proposition! Christian meditation, in contrast, always has in mind to fill a mind with God's truth. Christian meditation picks up where Eastern meditation leaves off. It builds on a cleared mind to fill it with God's voice.

CHAPTER 2

MEDITATION AND THE MIND

Who has put wisdom in the mind?
Or who has given understanding to the heart?
Job 38:36, NKJV

Meditation is an exercise of the mind. In order to understand how meditation works, a brief understanding of the mind is necessary. The Bible does not use precise language when describing the nature of the mind, neither does it provide a concise listing of all the operations of the mind. The Bible does, however present a rich variety of terms that help us understand this important part of our identity.

Lebh is a general term used in the Old Testament to describe various aspects of our intellectual and emotional nature. Nephesh is commonly understood as "soul" but is translated by "mind" in Deut. 18:6 (KJV). Ruah, a term commonly understood as "spirit", is translated "mind" in Gen. 26:35.

The fluid meanings of these three Hebrew terms is associated with the English word "mind". They indicate a rather large group of functions. Heart, soul, spirit, emotions, thinking, and the organ of communication with God are some of the many descriptive terms employed to describe the functions of the mind according to the Old Testament.

As early as Genesis we find the Patriarchs engaging in meditation. Isaac "went out to the field one evening to meditate" (Gen. 24:63 NIV). After the death of Moses, God instructed Joshua to give careful thought to the Law of God. He was to "meditate on it day and night" (Josh. 1:8 NIV).

The Psalmist frequently refers to meditation. He meditates on the unfailing love of God in the temple (48:9) and on the works and mighty deeds of God (77:12). Psalm 119 mentions meditation at least eight times taking as the subject things such as the precepts of God (v. 15, 78), the decrees of God (v. 23, 48), the wonders of God (v. 27), the Law of God (v. 97), the statutes of God (v. 99) and the promises of God (v. 148). The Psalmist meditates on the past works of God from "days long ago" (143:5).

Finally, the Psalmist declares his intention to meditate on the wonderful works of God (145:5).

The Hebrew word ŝîah means to "rehearse," "repent," or "go over a matter in one's mind." It is used of silent reflection or contemplation (Ps. 9:12; 77:8; 119:15, 23, 48, 78, 148). If one is suffering from emotional or physical pain, the translation of the word changes to "complain" (Job 7:11; Ps.55:17). Ŝîah is the key word in Psalm 77. The "complaint" (v. 3) of the Psalmist comes from his "contemplation" (v. 6) that God seems to be absent from him compared to days in the past. Yet the Psalmist determines to "meditate" (v. 6, 12) on the good works of God and "remember" (v. 10, 11) how the people of God were led through the wilderness by His mighty hand.

In the New Testament there are three Greek words that account for nearly all of the occurrences of the English word "mind". Much as terms in the Old Testament, these terms overlap in meaning and are not precise descriptions of different functions of the mind. They convey such ideas as understanding, thought, mind and reason.

Nous is a Greek word translated as "mind". It is the seat of all intellectual and emotional activity for both the saved and the unsaved. For Paul, the inner man becomes transformed by the renewing of the mind (naos, Rom 12:2). The mind is not an isolated organ, but is integrally connected with all of the functions of personality and being.

Another word is found in the New Testament with a somewhat more distinct meaning. Dianoia is literally translated as "meditation" or "reflection". It can describe a renewed mind in communion with God and an ability to know Christ as in Rom 12:2. It can also describe in a bad sense the thinking of the Gentiles who are "...walking in vanity of mind (nous) and a darkened understanding (dianoia)" (Eph 4:18).

The third word is sunesis. This term is used for an understanding that is enlightened from God: "The Lord give thee understanding (sunesis) in all things" (2 Tim. 2:7 KJV).

One theory suggests that the mind is neither good nor bad. It is viewed as neutral and impartial. Such a view presumes that any mind is capable of thinking pure thoughts. The New Testament does not view the mind this way. In the New Testament, the mind falls into one of two categories: evil or good. The evil mind is described as "hardened" (2 Cor. 3:14), "blinded" (2 Cor. 4:4), "depraved" (2 Tim. 3:8), or "debased" (Rom. 1:28). The good mind is described as "renewed" (Rom. 12:2) and "pure" (2 Pet. 3:1). The good mind loves God with its whole existence (Matt. 22:37; Mark 12:30; Luke 10:27). "The mind of Christ" is a possible reality for the Christian (1 Cor. 2:16). The good mind is the soil in which are planted of the Laws of God (Heb. 8:10). In this sense the mind is required to undergo transformation before it can be considered "good". Here is how Paul described it to the Romans:

"The mind of sinful man is death, but the mind controlled by the Spirit is life and peace; the sinful mind is hostile to God. It does not submit to God's law, nor can it do so. Those controlled by the sinful nature cannot please God" (Rom. 8:6-8 NIV).

The mind is a large part of who we are as individuals. It should not be thought of in the same terms as other individual organs such as our brain, liver or appendix. We cannot identify the exact location of where the mind exists. It is connected to the biblical terms "heart","soul" and "spirit." Defining exactly where the mind exists is not a possibility from biblical descriptions. The fluid language of the biblical terms leaves us with the impression that the mind is more of an aggregate of many functions and processes. Electricity has no form, it has no shape in and of itself. It uses the conductive properties of other things such as copper wires and light switches. Electricity flows as a kind of power that can act on things like motors or light bulbs. We must understand the mind in such a way. It is not identifiable as an organ or substance, but the power of the mind acts on us in profound ways.

Functions of the Mind

As we have seen from the Old and New Testaments, "mind" is a term which describes many diverse functions. It should not be understood as a compartment separate from the spirit, soul, emotions, intellect and will. More than 2,500 years ago a philosopher described the mind as an aggregate. He asked one of his followers which part of a chariot should be described as the chariot? Was the axel the chariot? Was the wheel the chariot? Was the compartment the chariot? He remarked that the mind likewise is an aggregate of parts. No one part can be called the mind by itself. It exists because its many parts function together.

Many attempts have been made to categorize the functions of the mind. For the sake of simplicity, I will refer to a group of five major functions that occur in the mind.

Consciousness

Our senses make contact with the world outside of us. With our eyes we see forms. Our ears hear sounds. We smell, taste and touch the physical world. These senses are like doorways that connect our mind to the outside world. These five senses gather information from the external world and our mind interprets that information. The mind itself acts as a kind of sixth sense. We can become conscious of things in our own minds. This information does not come through any of the five outer-senses. This is an inner-sense. It is aware of things like dreams and visions. This inner-sense can become aware of things happening within our mind itself. At the stage of bare consciousness, there is no "like" or "dislike". We do not categorize or rationalize the information gathered. We simply become aware of objects, sounds, tastes, smells, textures and ideas. This is a bare consciousness that is not yet connected to feelings or judgments.

Memory

Our mind has the amazing ability to store up thoughts and later recall them. What we were conscious of this morning or 50 years ago can be recalled with amazing accuracy. We all have vivid memories of things that happened many years ago. Memory works both as a deliberate process and a passive process. We can recall the thoughts we want to remember. The mind can also arbitrarily recall thoughts and we may find ourselves becoming conscious of a memory we did not intend to remember. Still, at this point our mind makes no judgments of the consciousness it has through memory.

Imagination

We can think of ideas that did not enter through our outer senses. We can deliberately put our mind to work to construct conscious thought based on nothing more than the thoughts themselves. We can imagine a world we have never experienced before. We can think of ourselves performing some great feat we have never physically tried. Imagination is the starting point for many great inventions. It can also be the beginning of a destructive process that keeps great things from being created.

Evaluation

Our mind can place many thoughts side by side and compare them. We create classifications of thoughts and file them according to criteria. We can examine thoughts for sensibility and reason. Our mind determines which thoughts are rational and which are not. Our mind can evaluate our own thoughts, but it can also import and evaluate the thoughts of others. Through this process we make generalizations such as "this thought makes sense," or "that thought is unbelievable and beyond consideration."

Estimation

At this stage, the mind takes the thoughts it has evaluated and begins to attach judgments to them. Ideas become "good" or "bad." Some thoughts become "pleasant" while others are viewed as "unpleasant." We create a system of personal likes and dislikes. We form a personal disposition through the activity of our mind. We say, "This is the way I am" to describe the results of this process. We form views and opinions about things. Some views are relatively unimportant to us. But other views we form are strongly held and we will go to great lengths to defend their legitimacy. Our minds go through a complex process over long periods of time to build judgments and preferences about things like religion, politics and ethics.

Each one of the functions of the mind is affected by sin. This brings a certain amount of darkness to each particular function. When sin affects our consciousness, it is darkened in such a way that we fail to perceive fully. The Psalmist reminds us time and again of the majesty of God through observing the physical creation. Yet how many times do we see the sunrise, sunset or majestic mountains and fail to recognize God's majesty? Our memory and imagination can be darkened such that we remember painful experiences more readily than pleasurable ones. We often imagine the worst even though there is no rational reason to do so. Darkness from sin can continue to our evaluations and estimations. We reason ourselves out of faith forgetting that "with God all things are possible." Our darkened opinions lead us to attitudes and emotions that are harmful to our progress as a child of God. The mind unaffected by the Holy Spirit is referred to as darkened, hostile and blinded. Let's revisit Paul's words in Romans 8:5-8:

"Those who live according to the sinful nature have their minds set on what that nature desires... The mind of sinful man is death... the sinful mind is hostile to God. It does not submit to God's law, nor can it do so. Those controlled by the sinful nature cannot please God" (NIV).

The process of salvation is more than a declaration of God that we are forgiven, cleansed and stand in a right position before Him. It is also a renewing process of our mind brought about by the power of the Holy Spirit. Every Christian undergoes an active process whereby the Holy Spirit causes them to "...be transformed by the renewing of your mind..." (Rom. 12:2 NIV). This is the process of allowing our mind to be "set on what the Spirit desires" and to be "controlled by the Spirit" (Rom. 8:5-6).

This process is ongoing throughout our lives as followers of Christ. The functions of our mind gradually become controlled by the Holy Spirit. When the Holy Spirit influences our mind, we can begin to understand the truth of God. Listen to what Paul tells the Corinthians about how their minds now work:

"So then, we do not speak in words taught by human wisdom, but in words taught by the Spirit, as we explain spiritual truths to those who have the Spirit. Whoever does not have the Spirit cannot receive the gifts that come from God's Spirit. Such a person really does not understand them; they are nonsense to him, because their value can be judged only on a spiritual basis. Whoever has the Spirit, however, is able to judge the value of everything, but no one is able to judge him. As the scripture says,

"Who knows the mind of the Lord?

Who is able to give him advice?"

We, however, have the mind of Christ"

(1Cor 2:13-16 TEV).

The mind is a complex system of processes that are continually working to provide us with awareness. The Bible is very descriptive of the many processes occurring in the mind. The terms "heart", "soul", "inner-man" "spirit" and "mind" are very close in nature and connected with the functions of the mind. We have identified five major functions of the mind. Consciousness is the mind's interpretation of the information gathered by the five senses. Consciousness can also come from the mind itself. Memory is the ability of the mind to store up thoughts. Imagination is the process of creating thoughts within the mind with no external information. Evaluation is the process of categorizing our thoughts into different classes such as "believable" or "not believable". Estimation is the attachment of judgments to our thoughts. As a result of this process thoughts become "good" or "bad." The mind forms the foundation for all of our personality, emotions, will and actions.

CHAPTER 3

MOTIVATIONS

*We...pray that [God will] fill your good ideas
and acts of faith with his own energy
so that it all amounts to something.*
2 Thessalonians 1:11, THE MESSAGE

The reason we act the way we do, whether good or bad, is the result of our motivations. Motivations are the result of our estimations. Motivations result when the mind goes through the five-step process described above. After an object or idea is classified and evaluated, certain feelings get attached to it. As those feelings are built up and stored in our mind they develop into predispositions and tendencies that make up our individual nature. We all have a unique personality that is the result of many years of mental processes. A large part of our personality is a set of emotions. If we are to understand why we do the things we do, we must understand the role of emotions and their limits, as well as how they influence our will and actions.

Emotions

Our emotions are the result of the functions of the mind. For example, let's say we become conscious of an individual. We see that their clothes are torn, and our nose detects a particular odor. This is function 1 of the mind's cycle. Next we recall things we have learned about such an individual. They are homeless. They are not very clean. We may recall a previous encounter or a story someone has told regarding such a person (step 2). Our mind moves on to consider possibilities and create scenarios of what might happen. Perhaps this person will try to manipulate, or steal from you; or worse (step 3). Next our mind places this person in a certain category of "undesirable people." We reason that it is best for us if we avoid such a person (step 4). Finally we construct opinions about not only this one individual, but all those like him. We perceive him as less desirable. Finally, we begin to develop feelings of distrust and disgust for people similar to him.

Only after the mind has completed the cycle of functions do we develop these emotional feelings. These feelings can become so strong that even the word "homeless" raises emotions of disgust. This cycle happens in an instant.

Sometimes the cycle results in no emotions. Sometimes very strong emotions result. These feelings are unique to each individual. Certain songs bring feelings as our mind remembers an event in our past. An odor can trigger emotions tied to our childhood. Feelings such as hatred, joy, peace, fear, sadness, contentment, anger, (the list is endless) all result from the operation of our individual mind.

Emotions are personal. Each person responds in a different way emotionally to the same stimulus. Emotions are not merely instinctual. If this were the case, we would all react in the same way emotionally, say, to the bark of a dog. But some people experience interest as the result of a dog bark. Some are drawn out of emotional attachment to dogs. Some are cautious and yet others are terrified. This range of emotions from a single dog bark is conditioned by past experiences and ideas reinforced over time. Each of us has our own emotional make-up that has developed as a result of our mind's activities.

Emotions are conditioned also by context. Music can evoke different emotions based on where it is heard. For example a love song can bring emotions of fondness and memories of tender moments spent with a special person. If, however, you are in church listening to a sermon and someone interrupts the message with the current hit country song, different emotions arise. The music is not appropriate in that situation. As a result emotions of tenderness are replaced by emotions of irritation (or perhaps relief if the sermon was not so good).

Emotions arise quickly. We do not always have the option of screening them before they motivate us. They also subside rather slowly. This results often in what we call displacement. For example if you are scolded by a boss at work, anger and perhaps embarrassment arise immediately. But because it is inappropriate to react outwardly at that time, you endure the confrontation—maybe even apologize—and go about your business. Later that evening you are confronted by your husband who asks why dinner is slow in being prepared. You immediately react with anger and tell him to cook his own food, or better yet go somewhere else and eat alone. Why the sudden outburst? Perhaps your husband was not as sensitive as he should of been, but his question did not alone prompt the kind of emotional response you gave. Emotions arise quickly and subside slowly. Things that happen to us create emotions that sometimes lay concealed until a later time.

Our feelings are very strong motivators. We often act based on how we feel. Fear motivates us to run away. Hatred motivates us to harm another. Greed motivates us to steal. It would be wrong to state that hatred makes me harm another, or greed makes me steal. We cannot blame our emotions for solely directing our actions. They are nothing more than feelings that have arisen because of our mind's processes. We do have certain control over our emotions. But acting contrary to our feelings is a very difficult thing. Even when we know something is right, we often lack the corage to do it because of fear. Or likewise, when we know something is wrong, we often lack the ability to stop ourselves because of feelings like desire for revenge or justification. We certainly need to allow the Holy Spirit to assist us in cleansing our feelings. This process is done as He influences our mind and brings transformation there.

Volition

Our volition, or will, results from many factors. Our emotions influence our will. I may not want to go to the dentist because I am afraid. Or I may have a strong desire to go to my parent's for my mother's cooking. Sometimes outside influences affect our volition. Demons can attack our mind with temptations. The strategy of Satan is to gain access and establish what Paul calls "strongholds" in our mind. The level of darkness based on demonic influence varies greatly from person to person. The Bible records less significant levels of demon influence resulting in doubt and ignorance. Such a case is Peter's sudden outburst in opposition to the Lord's statement of his coming death (Matt. 16:22). In extreme cases, like the Gadarene demoniac

(Mark 5:2-5), the will of the individual is directed by the presence of demonic forces.

The influence of demons does not destroy the will of a person. They exercise a level of control over it. We cannot say that we have "no will of our own." What we want results from the manner in which our minds have been influenced. Even Jesus was subject to influences that affected his will. While in the Garden of Gethsamene Jesus expressed that He did not want to die as a substitute for sinful mankind. His will stood in contrast to the will of His Father as he said, "...not My will, but Yours be done" (Luke 22:42 Emphasis mine). Here we see two distinct wills. Jesus had subjected himself to human existence. Jesus, the human man, was influenced by the things in and around the physical realm. The will of the Father was to see the completion of the plan of salvation by grace that He initiated even before the creation of the world (Eph. 1:4). The will of Jesus was different from the will of the Father, but Jesus subjected His will and became obedient, even to dying on the cross.

Psychologists call some parts of our will "instinctual". They claim that we have little control over the influence they exhibit in our lives. Things like physical survival, nourishment and sex have been understood in such a manner. But the Bible teaches us that we do have potential control over every part of our volition . Jesus overcame the will to avoid crucifixion and went willingly to the cross. In time many of the Apostles died a martyr's death, overcoming the instinct of physical survival. We are taught to develop our spiritual health through the discipline of fasting. Going without food as a deliberate choice that exercises our control over the desire to eat. We are commanded to avoid all sex outside of the marriage commitment. In spite of the natural will to procreate, it is forbidden by God except in marriage. For the Apostle Paul, sex was avoided altogether. His celibate lifestyle was an expression of his dedication to God (1 Cor. 7:7). Our will is not laid helpless at the mercy of outside forces such as emotions, demons and instinct.

Willfulness is determined by several motivating factors that are developed in our mind. As our mind functions, our personal will is developed based on how much light or darkness has influenced our thoughts. For example, if a person engages their mind on dark thoughts of greed they will develop volition to steal. If a person engages their mind in lustful thoughts through consciousness (pictures, movies), memory, or imagination, they will develop a will to commit adultery. If a person allows his mind to dwell on dark ideas of racism and bigotry through comparison and opinions, volition will be developed to avoid or even do harm to those who are different. The opposite is also true. If a person has sufficiently considered the teachings of Jesus about caring for the needy, and they encounter a homeless person, feelings of compassion can arise followed by the desire to give. If a person thinks enough about the teachings of Jesus concerning loving our enemies, feelings of hatred and bitterness can subside and our desires for their harm can be changed into willingness for their well-being.

Our will and emotions are strong motivators. In fact, most people act based on the direction of emotions and will alone. "Of course" you say, "what other motivators are there?" There are in fact many motivations outside of our will and emotions. Satan's strategy is to bring motivation to do wrong. He gains access through our mind. He uses the functions of the mind to plant seeds that grow into volitions to do wrong. He uses our eyes, ears, memory and imagination to start the process of imposing his motivations on us. Once a motivation is planted in our mind it awaits the perfect time to rise and influence our thought process. This process can either be arrested or encouraged by us. We can agree with the motivations of Satan or we can identify and reject them. In this sense Satan really has no power of us unless we agree with his motivations.

Actions

Emotion and volition unite to form motivation which results in specific actions. A person who has a hot temper and lashes out with abusive words and violence does so because of strong emotional and volitional motivations. We can identify emotions of hatred and fear in such people, whether they admit them or not. We can also see how those feelings motivate a volition to cause harm. Together the feelings and will form a strong motivation that directs his actions towards verbal and physical abuse.

Actions, whether they are good or bad, are influenced by emotions and volition. These motivations are the result of the operations of our mind. In this sense, the mind is the foundation for all actions. For those who live separated from the grace of God, Paul describes their minds as "darkened," making their thoughts "futile." They are separated from the life of God because of "ignorance" in them due to the "hardening of their hearts" (Eph 4:17-24 NIV). The result of this kind of mind is a loss of all sensitivity for what is right. The conscience is made unconscious and ignored. The result is a life of ever-increasing deeds that displease God and destroys others.

Paul explains the utter hopelessness of a person who is bound by a dark, sinful mind by declaring emphatically that they are "...unable to please God" (Rom. 8:8). The motivations created by the natural mind outside of God's grace are too strong to be overcome by human nature alone. There may be some degree of conscience that attempts to guide the actions in some form of morality, but this conscience in the darkened mind is tainted at best. For the most part, the darkened mind ignores the conscience to the extent that it becomes silent. This silent conscience no longer steers the individual into any real meaningful moral system. Occasionally, through much effort, a darkened mind may develop a moral code and follow it with some dedication. But this is not the normal experience of a darkened mind.

How can any of us be free from darkness? Paul asks the question this way in Roman 7, "who will rescue me from this body of death?" In short, we are "to be made new in the attitude of our minds" (Eph. 4:23). To change our actions, our mind must function in a different manner. It is the transforming work of the Holy Spirit that enables a change in the nature of my emotions and volition.

If we are going to act in a way that is pleasing to God, we must conform our will to His will, just as Jesus did in the Garden of Gethsamene. Jesus acted in a manner pleasing to God in spite of the motivations of emotions and volition that influenced Him to do otherwise. This is accomplished through allowing our minds to be transformed by the Holy Spirit who actively works to dispel darkness and conform our mind to the mind of Christ.

The motivation of emotions and volition is strong. Much of what we do is the result of how these two motivations have formed in our mind over time.

Once God brings the touch of saving grace into our minds things begin to change. But as a result of God's grace, we are given yet another motivation. This motivation can overcome the strongest emotion. It can lead us to act in a way pleasing to God against our own will to do otherwise. We will next turn our attention to the strongest motivation of all: faith.

CHAPTER 4

FAITH

"Look at that man, bloated by self-importance —
full of himself but soul-empty. But the person in
right standing before God through loyal and steady
believing is fully alive, really alive.

Habakkuk 2:4, THE MESSAGE

Faith is not something we create in the mind. Faith is the result of the Holy Spirit's influence on our minds. Faith is a state of the mind that has been transformed by the Holy Spirit. Even though faith does not originate in the mind, it is not a separate function from the mind. The mind is the object of faith. When faith comes to a person, it begins its work on the mind and it operates from the mind. Once faith transforms the functions of the mind, our emotions and volition are further made to line up with faith. Faith can be the sole motivator for our actions if we learn the discipline of exercising it. A little faith is a powerful force; able to move mountains and bring miracles into existence. Let's put faith to work on what we already know about the functions of the mind. How does faith change it all?

The supreme biblical example of faith is described as existing in Abraham (Heb. 11:1-12). Faith illustrated by Abraham was a strong reliance upon God who he knew to be trustworthy. Such reliance enabled Abraham to treat the future as present and the invisible as seen. God promised Abraham that his descendants would be as numerous as the sand on the seashore. Considering both he and his wife were long past the childbearing age, this faith was remarkable. We can see how the faith of Abraham affected every part of his mind, emotions volition and actions. In short, faith rose to be the supreme motivator in Abraham's life.

Faith-Consciousness

Paul tells the Corinthian Christians, "we live by faith, not by sight" (2Cor. 5:7). Our awareness of the world as perceived through our senses is not ultimate reality. Sometimes our eyes cannot be trusted. Faith can bring us into awareness of the ultimate realities of God in a way our senses cannot. Hebrews 11:1 expresses the nature of faith as the "evidence of things not seen." A faith-consciousness has an awareness of God's reality that outweighs the immediate reality gathered by our senses. If our eyes fail to see, our faith provide "sight" into God's truth. Abraham was still living by faith at the time of his death. He had not received all that god had promised; yet he "saw them and welcomed them from a distance" (Heb 11:13). When faith influences our consciousness reality changes for us. What God has promised now becomes a greater reality than what we see, hear, smell, taste and feel. Like Abraham, we know God's promises are to be believed and His reality is the most sure of all.

Faith-Memory

When Abraham received the promise from God that his descendants would be as great as the stars in the sky, he was already more than 65 years old. His son Isaac was born 35 years later, when he was more than 100. During the time before the birth of Isaac, the faith of Abraham endured peaks and valleys. There were several interventions by God to help Abraham remember the promise he had been given. Aided by faith, Abraham kept the promise alive for more than 30 years until the birth of his son Isaac. Abraham was able to look ahead and see the future as a reality because of his ability to recall the memory of the promise of God. Again, Abraham left his home country and settled in a foreign land.

He lived in tents as a stranger, though he knew God had promised to give him that land as an inheritance. The memory of God's promise enabled Abraham to look ahead and know the future. "For he was looking forward to the city with foundations, whose architect and builder is God" (Heb. 11:10). Our memory is an important part of our life of faith. God's promises stay alive as we recall them by faith.

Faith-Imagination

It must have taken some time for Abraham to truly imagine in his mind the promise God made to him. The mental picture of his descendants numbering as stars in the heavens and sand on the seashore demanded Abraham engage his imagination in a way that relied on faith. Sarah had less ability to exercise a faith-imagination, for when she heard the promise from her husband she laughed at the absurdity of it all.

Paul speaks of a hidden wisdom given to us by God. This wisdom has the task of engaging our imagination to perceive the goodness of God's blessings. "No eye has seen, no ear has heard, no mind has conceived what God has prepared for those who love him— but God has revealed it to us by his Spirit" (1Cor. 2:9). When the rational and conscious portions of the mind fail to comprehend, God can energize our faith-imagination to somehow conceive of the profound and abundant goodness of God.

Faith-Evaluation

As Abraham thought about the promise God had given him, he determined that what God had said must be believed. His evaluation of the promise was founded on his understanding of God. Whatever God has promised, that ought to be believed. Abraham "was enabled to become a father because he considered him faithful who had made the promise" (Heb. 11:11). When faith influences our evaluation process we are able to position certain thoughts to be believed even in the face of doubt from natural reason. Abraham determined that God's promise was believable in the face of physical logic that declared offspring an impossibility. This is the effect of faith on our evaluation process: we believe based on God's reputation and truth above any other. Even after God gave instructions to Abraham to sacrifice his promised son, the faith-evaluation in him reasoned that "God could raise the dead" (Heb. 11:19).

Faith-Estimation

In this level of thinking, our minds are "set" with determination and resolve. Faith is "being sure of what we hope for" (Heb. 11:1). It is said of the ancient saints of faith that "...they were longing for a better country — a heavenly one" (Heb. 11:16).

This longing is the result of the Holy Spirit influencing their estimation process. After evaluating we begin to attach importance to the things of God. We attach "goodness" to what God wants for us. We establish priorities of what we desire most. This process was alive in the Apostle Paul as he considered that everything was "...a loss compared to the surpassing greatness of knowing Christ Jesus my Lord" (Phil. 3:8). Further he declares, "I want to know Christ and the power of his resurrection and the fellowship of sharing in his sufferings" (Phil. 3:10). As the process of estimation is influenced by the Holy Spirit, we begin to see changes in our emotions and our volition. We can be at peace instead of uptight. We can desire to do what is pleasing to God.

In short, the phrase in Hebrews 11:1, "faith is being sure of what we hope for and certain of what we do not see," is parallel in form to our familiar saying, "Knowledge is power." Faith is designed to influence the way our mind works. It is the key to how the Holy Spirit transforms our mind. God desires faith to become the strongest motivation in our lives. It is through faith that we can believe the impossible. Through faith we can see the invisible. We can have hope and peace in a dark world through faith. Faith is the sole element that inspires us to reach beyond what is humanly possible. It causes us to be satisfied with only what is ultimately good. It is only through the influence of faith that we aspire to the position of "child of God" and experience all that implies.

Since the mind is central to faith, it is sensible for us to cultivate our minds in order to create an atmosphere in which faith can grow. We spend so much time looking after our physical bodies and our physical possessions, we seldom have time left in the day to look after the progress of our faith.

This is why meditation is so vital. It focuses the mind to allow the Holy Spirit to dispel the darkness and bring transformation through establishing faith. Let's say one morning you enter the kitchen and notice a glass on the counter. At first you have only a superficial knowledge. You are aware of little more than the general description of "glass." But if you direct your attention to the glass and approach for a closer look we will see quite a lot more. You notice that the glass still has some liquid in it. You also notice lipstick on the rim. Through your sense of smell you guess "orange juice." A taste confirms it—fresh-squeezed. You assume it was your wife, or perhaps your daughter that drank the juice. But in order to know the truth further insight is required. We might call this "investigation." Experts can lift fingerprints and extract DNA from the glass and can compare it to known samples telling exactly who was drinking out of the glass. Now there are no guesses, no doubts. Your wife was the one drinking from the glass. This is the role of faith according to

Hebrews 12:1. It is evidence. It is substance. It is meant to eliminate all doubt and reveal the true nature of things.

There are different levels of perception. A superficial cognition yields but a few facts. If we focus our attention we can learn more facts. But only though expert analysis can we become intimately aware of something as it really is. Faith is the motivation that keeps us examining the world around us. Without it we simply get a general view, a superficial appreciation of how things really are. But through faith we can come to know things in their true nature. It is a matter of using our faith and exercising faith's ability to direct our mind. If the saying is true, "knowledge is power," then it is absolutely true that "knowledge through faith is ultimate power."

Faith as a motivation leads us to discover the truth and act in ways pleasing to God, often in spite of our emotions and will. It is nice when our emotions are godly, but that is not a consistent reality in this sinful world. The same is true of our will. It is nice when I want to pray, be generous and love my enemy, but it is more often a wish than a reality. Faith is God's gift to motivate us to please Him in spite of everything else. We can ill afford to neglect the home of our faith: the mind.

Meditation is an opportunity for faith to transform our minds. It is true that faith is able to influence us anywhere at any time, but meditation provides an "improved environment" for faith to direct our perception. Through mediation we quiet the mind from distraction and deliberately prepare it to receive the transforming power of faith. If we allow faith to prosper in our minds in this way, it will bring increased pleasure to God (because without faith it is impossible to please God) and increased possibility to us (because faith is the substance of things hoped for).

CHAPTER 5

DEFINING MEDITATION

Meditate within your heart on your bed, and be still.

Psalm 4:4, NKJV

The Century Dictionary defines meditation as "a private devotional act, consisting in deliberate reflection or contemplation upon some spiritual truth or mystery, accompanied by mental prayer and by acts of the affection and of the will, especially formation of resolutions as to future conduct."

Take one minute and think about a butterfly. It moves from one flower to another. It extracts only nectar that is quickly and easily accessible. It never rests long at one place. It flutters about in an unpredictable manner. The mind naturally works in the same manner. It wanders and flits about like a butterfly in search of nectar. One moment this thought arises. Soon another thought comes to the front of our consciousness. We fail to concentrate for any length of time on one particular subject. We are in a constant cycle of moving from one thought to another—some conscious and some unconscious. We have all been annoyed at someone who cannot concentrate long enough to communicate a single complete thought. Or we have been frustrated with ourselves when we sit down to read and cannot recall the details of the page we have just read!

Meditation is an exercise which trains the mind to remain fixed on one subject for an extended period of time. For a start, many of you will feel as if five minutes is an eternity to fix your attention solely on one subject. But after some time you will develop skills that will enable you to stay focused and concentrate for much longer periods. It is quite easy for someone skilled in meditation to contemplate several hours on a single subject with little or no mental distraction. It is in this kind of meditation that the Holy Spirit can do his deepest work in our lives. Stillness and rest from mental distraction is a gift we give the Holy Spirit. But because it is difficult, we seldom find the time or energy, so the Holy Spirit often resorts to the next best thing and speaks to us in our sleep! Through meditation we focus our minds and give time to God to renew us by transforming our minds.

Meditation is not prayer. Prayer is communication with God largely through the spoken word. Prayer is concerned with confession, supplication and intercession. The goal of prayer involves direct address to God. Meditation is not worship. Though we may be in an attitude of worship, we are not actively giving outward praise or adoration to God. Meditation is not study. Study is engaging the mind to learn facts and principles. Study involves business of reading and cross-referencing. The goal of study is to learn by feeding our intellect information. Meditation is not receiving revelation. Our goal in meditation is not to receive a new and unique revelation of a particular truth. Although this may happen, the goals and nature of meditation are more humble.

Characteristics of Meditation

Meditation consists of at least three major characteristics: it is inward, silent and purposeful. By inward we mean that all of our attention is focused on our own mind and how it works. Unlike prayer and worship, we are not primarily concerned with God's character. Unlike study we are not trying to gain understanding of someone else's mind. We are focusing attention on our own mind in order to understand ourselves. This will create discipline that will aid the Holy Spirit's task of instilling greater faith.

By silent we mean just that. There is no mantra or repeated phrases necessary to meditate. Many meditation disciplines teach chanting mantras, but they are unnecessary and often distract from the simple process of quietness. Remember that the Holy Spirit is aiding the process, so traditional formulas and non-Christian methods of gaining "centeredness" are unnecessary.

By purposeful we mean that meditation has three specific goals. Meditation's first goal is to become aware of yourself—body, mind and emotions. Secondly, meditation quiets your mind to receive God's truth. It is not a complicated process. We are merely creating a clean page on which the Holy Spirit can be free to communicate to us. Third, meditation prepares us for what lies ahead of us. Since none of us knows with absolute certainty what lies ahead in a day, we can prepare ourselves to respond in faith to any situation we may face. Meditation recalls the past through becoming aware of our body and mind. It focuses on the present as we allow the Holy Spirit to transform us. And it prepares us for future encounters of the day.

Steps For Meditation

What are the steps of meditation? Seven steps of meditation are explained below. Each step is preparation for the next. It is like climbing a mountain, experiencing the summit and returning to the place where wthr climb began. As you familiarize yourself with the overall principles of meditation, you will be able to pay less attention to the steps and exercise some latitude. In this way you will develop your own style of meditation. The steps are:

1. Body awareness

2. Mind Awareness

3. God Awareness

4. Truth Encounter

5. God Awareness

6. Mind Awareness

7. Body Awareness

Preparation and posture

The place you meditate is not as important as you might think. The goal of meditation is to discipline the mind to concentrate on things that are deliberately chosen. This means that if there are subtle distractions or interruptions it really will not make any difference because you can discipline your mind to concentrate even in a setting that is non-peaceful. Even so, to begin with it will be necessary to choose a place relatively free from distraction. The Psalmist discloses several times that his meditation is done on his bed. This is perhaps a good place to start. Late in the evening just before going to sleep is an excellent time to meditate. Your mind will be full of thoughts and memories from the busy day. You will find yourself enjoying a much deeper and restful sleep if you calm your mind and focus before retiring for the day.

Because meditation is a discipline and requires effort, the best posture is probably not in the lying position. Sitting on the bed with your legs crossed and back straight, is a comfortable yet alert position. Your hand positions are not important. Just find a comfortable place for them to rest. Once you settle on a position, try not to move unnecessarily. You will find that your physical comfort is largely a function of your thought processes. If you are uncomfortable at the start of your meditation, you will find that often you become more comfortable once you begin the process, even without having to move frequently.

Meditation is a specific discipline of exercising our mind. It is not identical to prayer, worship, study or receiving unique revelation. Meditation is an inward concentration that focuses our mind with the goal of letting the Holy Spirit cleanse the past, influence the present and consecrate us for the future. As a discipline it requires attention and effort. Physical exercise results in improved health for the body. In the same way, meditation results in increased transformation of the mind.

CHAPTER 6

STEPS 1-3: CONDITIONED BY THE PAST

*I am focusing all my energies on this one thing:
Forgetting the past and looking forward to what lies
ahead*
Philippians 3:13, NLT

Step 1: Body-Awareness.

The first step in meditation is to begin the process
of becoming aware. We start with the body because
it is easy to be conscious of our own body. The first
step is to focus on your breathing. Do not change it
intentionally, just become aware of the in and out
breaths. Recall that the life of Adam was breathed
into him by God (Gen. 1:21). God's Spirit is known
as "breath". After a few minutes of focusing your
mind on your breathing, let your mind become

aware of your physical body. Start in the center, around your abdomen and concentrate on how you are feeling. Move outward toward your arms and legs noticing any tension or pain. The purpose of this exercise is to get our mind to systematically focus on individual parts of our body. In doing so we are directing our mind as a discipline.

The transformation of our bodies is a past, present and future reality. We have been changed in a profound way by the grace of God. Paul describes us as "new creations" in Jesus Christ (2 Cor. 5:17). This extends beyond our soul and spirit. Our bodies have been cleansed enabling us access to God's presence. "Let us draw near to God with a sincere heart in full assurance of faith, having our hearts sprinkled to cleanse us from a guilty conscience and having our bodies washed with pure water" (Heb. 10:22 NIV). The past transformation of our bodies is real. As a child of God you have already been transformed.

This transformation is ongoing in the present. We are to act in faith to present our bodies to God as living sacrifices (Rom. 12:1). Our mind must continually be aware that we are not self-owned, we are purchased by God and as his possessions we are expected to honor Him with our bodies (1 Cor. 6:20). Use this time to consider what God expects from us with regard to our body:

"Therefore do not let sin reign in your mortal body so that you obey its evil desires. Do not offer the parts of your body to sin, as instruments of wickedness, but rather offer yourselves to God, as those who have been brought from death to life; and offer the parts of your body to him as instruments of righteousness... For if you live according to the sinful nature, you will die; but if by the Spirit you put to death the misdeeds of the body, you will live" (Rom. 6:12-13; 8:13NIV).

"Do you not know that your body is a temple of the Holy Spirit, who is in you, whom you have received from God? You are not your own; you were bought at a price. Therefore honor God with your body" (1Cor. 6:19-20 NIV).

These verses express the ownership and rights of God to tell us what we may and may not do with our bodies. We are to consider our body the tool of God through which He can show himself to the world. Our holy lifestyle is a reflection of God's holiness. Our turning away from sin is a powerful declaration of the nature of God and His holy expectation for all people.

Not only is transformation past and present, it is also future. God is not finished with the process of changing our body. And He will not be finished until we perfectly resemble the nature and glory of Christ in our body. God's perfect will is that our body comes under His control where His power can transform. And he will transform our bodies. Christ's power "will transform our lowly bodies so that they will be like his glorious body (Phil. 3:21).

Body awareness will assist us in making positive changes in both our attitude and actions associated with our physical body. Our actions matter. We should not think lightly of the value of our body. We certainly should not squander and cheapen what God paid such a high price for. Let this time of body awareness be used by God to remind you of past actions that displeased Him. Perhaps a change in lifestyle or diet is a part of God's plan for you. Your physical health is related to your spiritual health. We cannot be healthy spiritually with faulty attitudes and thoughts concerning our physical body. Keep aware of the memories that arise of your sinful activities. Keep them in your conscious mind. We will deal with those deeds in a moment.

Step 2: Mind-Awareness.

Becoming aware of the activity of our mind is a little more difficult than body awareness. The actions of our body happen slowly. The mind, however is ablaze with lightening speed. It zips from one thought to another. After spending some time focusing on body-awareness, you have slowed the extreme jumping around of your mind from one thought to another. Now we will go one step farther and focus on the thoughts and memories we have stored up.

If this is your first time in meditation, you will have memories not only of the days thoughts, but memories from long ago coming to the front of your consciousness. Do not try to stop them. Try to understand the nature of those memories. Since this is an exercise in building faith, it may be that The Holy Spirit is bringing those particular memories to the surface so you can deal with them.

Become aware of the thoughts and emotions surrounding the memories that arise. Realize that we all have lies stored up inside of us. They sometimes come to the surface along with a memory we recall. These lies usually are associated with unpleasant feelings like guilt, fear or anger. These lies can surface as thoughts like, "I am a bad person" ,"God is mad at me," or "God will not forgive me." Our thinking needs to become free of these lies and others like them. If we have honestly sought God's forgiveness we should not feel guilty or ashamed (Rom. 8:1). Paul says that we must "...demolish arguments and every pretension that sets itself up against the knowledge of God, and we take captive every thought to make it obedient to Christ (2 Cor. 10:5 NIV). Realize that if there are a great deal of negative thoughts and emotions rising in your mind, it may be because of unconfessed sin. Another cause may be that someone repeatedly reinforced the lies in your mind by telling you over and over again that you were going to fail, or that your were not a good person, or that you were not smart, or not pretty.

Recall the kinds of thoughts your mind has had recently. But do not let yourself recall only bad thoughts. You have also been engaging in Godly thoughts as well. If you become aware of thought patterns that are harmful to your spiritual health, make yourself conscious of them, we will deal with those in a moment.

Step 3: God-Awareness.

Now that we have taken some time to develop both body and mind-awareness, there are undoubtedly some disturbing things that have revealed themselves. We may be aware of actions done and thoughts entertained that need to be cleansed. We will deal with those things as we concentrate on the closeness of God.

First, begin to expand your thinking beyond your body and mind to the center of your being. The

Holy Spirit has taken up residence inside you. The presence of the Holy Spirit is present to affect the work of salvation in your mind and body. We are sons and daughters of God. God has determined to buy us back from slavery to sin. He accomplished this through sending Jesus to die for us, as a ransom for our freedom. God sent the Spirit of his Son into our hearts, the Spirit who calls out, "Abba, Father." So you are no longer a slave, but a son; and since you are a son, God has made you also an heir" (Gal. 4:6-7 NIV). God does not want to punish you for the deeds and thoughts that have arisen in your mind. He wants to cleanse them and bring transformation. He wants us to be free from those deeds and thoughts; and also free from the lies that are associated with them. The kinds of thoughts that naturally arise in us are conditioned by the past. Our experiences and imaginations set the stage for the kinds of thoughts that will emerge later. We need to destroy the foundation of the lies and create a foundation for the truth.

Take a moment and recall the sinful deeds and thoughts that have arisen in your mind during this exercise. Silently ask God to forgive you. Let images arise in your mind of God's forgiveness. Become aware of the peace of God as it descends on you. Notice the weight of sin as it lifts from your body and mind. In Jesus "we have redemption through his blood, the forgiveness of sins, in accordance with the riches of God's grace that he lavished on us with all wisdom and understanding (Eph. 1:7-8 NIV). You may even be aware of physical changes as the forgiveness of God is realized. You may relax, breathing may slow, or a smile may come to your face.

The first three steps of our meditation focuses on the past. As we focus on body-awareness we recall failures of our actions. Through mind-awareness we remember thoughts that are displeasing to God. Through God-awareness we allow the forgiving grace of God to cleanse us. This cleansing is complete and prepares our mind for the next step in our meditation: truth-encounter.

CHAPTER 7

STEP 4: CONTROLLED BY THE PRESENT

*Those of us who are strong and able in the faith
need to step in and lend a hand to those who falter,
and not just do what is most convenient for us.
Strength is for service, not status. Each one of us
needs to look after the good of the people around
us, asking ourselves, "How can I help?"*

Romans 15:1-2, THE MESSAGE

You might be thinking, "This is simple." Yes, on one hand the process of meditating is simple. Remember, however, that what we are after is the continued and deliberate control of our mind. Through the process so far, your mind has probably wandered several times. When this happens, keep refocusing it as many times as you need to.

Up to this point we have been developing awareness that has been conditioned by the past. The goal has been to eliminate some obstacles that stand in the way of letting the Holy Spirit reveal His truth to us. The next step for us is to focus our mind in order to encounter the truth of God. The Bible gives us many subjects we may meditate on: The works of creation (Gen. 1-3); the character of God (Deut 32:4); the work of Christ (Heb 12:2-3); the nature of the Holy Spirit (John 15-16); the promises of God's words (Ps 119); the value and immortality of our soul (Mark 8:36); the grace of God in our salvation, to name a few.

We can use visual images or portions of scripture to aid us. The chapter on Meditation Helps has several aids to assist you as you develop your skills. Realize, however, that you do not necessarily need any helps. You will eventually develop the skill to focus on a truth that comes from the Holy Spirit Himself.

Temptation Killers

There are a few meditation-killers that should be guarded against to make meditation effective. You must avoid these temptations and refuse to follow where they want to lead you. The first is the temptation to study. This is not the time to search your Bible encyclopedia for background information. No matter how strong the urge to look up information, don't do it. Keep your mind focused on the subject at hand without giving in to the urge to expand your knowledge of the subject. In short, this exercise is not to learn anything new, but to become more keenly aware of what we already know. Think of your mind as a piece of fabric immersed in dye. In order for the colors to be vibrant, what is needed is more time in the dye, not necessarily more dye itself.

The second meditation killer is thinking that you already know the subject thoroughly enough. We kill our meditation when we think, "I already know about that." There is benefit in meditating on God's grace, or the nature of the incarnation, or the value of the human soul even if you consider yourself an expert on the subject. There are facets of truth that lay hidden from us until we take the time to contemplate them over a period of time. The more time we spend in meditation on a particular subject, the deeper our awareness can be of that subject. I say "awareness" as opposed to "knowledge" because, again, the goal is not to learn more knowledge, but to keep what we already know at the front of our mind throughout the day in ways that changes how we think and act. This is how transformation happens.

The third meditation killer is expecting a life-changing revelation of new, unique truth. Do not entertain the idea that the goal of meditation is get a unique revelation that no one else has ever understood. Thinking this way will engage your imagination in a way that will prove to be counter-productive to what the Holy Spirit wants to do. If we are expecting flashes of lightening and visions of the third heavens we are disengaging from the purpose of simple meditation.

Truth Encounter

From the many scriptural subjects that can be meditated on, the best are commonly known and simple truths—God's law (already revealed), the past miracles of God (already known), promises of God (already heard) — you get my point. When we fix our attention on getting a new unique revelation we automatically categorize the old truths we already know as less important. This is not a healthy aspiration for the mind of a Christian. Seeking to know new and unique truth continually leads to compromising the simple truths through neglect and abusing our faith by overemphasizing ideas that are often as much human imagination as Godly revelation. Just remember that as exciting as a new and unique revelation is, the priority remains that "we must be sure to obey the truth we have learned already" (Phil. 3:16 NLT).

Avoiding the three meditation killers is the first step to a truth encounter. We must do all we can to give the Holy Spirit a clean page on which to write. Our minds must first be free of all notions of directing the Holy Spirit or presuming to know the kinds of things He will say.

Truth encounter requires a different kind of mental skill than awareness meditation. In awareness meditation, memory is the primary function. Thoughts and acts are simply brought to the front of your mind. In truth encounter, memory needs to be "turned off" and a new function initiated to engage the mind.

Turn to a page in the section on meditation helps and focus your mind on the whole page. Read the scripture through, focusing on each and every word of the passage. Read the passage only once, but take your time in doing so. Now close your eyes and recall as much of the passage as possible. Keep your eyes closed and resist entertaining any meditation-killers. Let the message sink in to your mind. It is not important that you remember every word of the passage. Keep your mind trained on the message of the passage. Do not let your mind wander too far off of the subject. If it does, gently bring it back to focus on the message you just read. Let questions arise in your mind, and then let the answer follow. Do not force your thinking. Let periods of mind-silence continue if you need to. Be aware of the different functions of the mind as they arise and diminish. When evaluation arises to answer one of the questions asked by your mind, keep it working, reasoning through each answer your mind presents. If imagination arises, keep aware of it and let it produce mental images in keeping with the subject. If emotions arise, keep awareness of them and also engage your evaluation to determine why those emotions are being initiated.

As you can see, the many different processes of the mind are rapid and dynamic, creating various thoughts, emotions and mental images. The goal of meditation at this level is to keep new thoughts in line with the subject arising while not letting the mind wander from the subject. You may find yourself straining at first, but it is important to relax. Your mind works incredibly well without any effort on your part. Simply keep your mind engaged on the subject and attempt to be aware of the many functions arising and diminishing.

It is important to keep your thoughts from being directed towards maintaining and fortifying your own personal views. We all have ideas about what we consider important biblical truths. Topics such as eschatology, work of the Holy Spirit, the nature of God, and others are taught with conviction. Our churches are not divided along cultural or social lines so much as along the lines of differing views. This is an unfortunate truth concerning the Christian church today. Meditation techniques soften the harsh edges of personal views. Through honest contemplation, our minds allow an opportunity to let other views gain honest influence in your mind.

Should we want the sharp edges of our convictions to be softened? In Romans 14, Paul is giving instruction about how to think about the differing views of others. These are not trivial subjects. Diet and holy days were held in high position. But neither were they matters of salvation. Paul is concerned that the weak in faith are not harmed by the insensitivity of those who held strong views. Interestingly, the weak in faith according to Paul are those who have the strongest religious views. "One man's faith allows him to eat everything, but another man, whose faith is weak, eats only vegetables (Rom. 14:2 NIV). The motivation for this dietary view was the fear that the Christian might eat meat that had been offered to idols. As a result, one prevailing view was that Christians should abstain from all meat. It is this stricter dietary view that Paul describes as weaker in faith.

"Therefore let us stop passing judgment on one another. Instead, make up your mind not to put any stumbling block or obstacle in your brother's way. As one who is in the Lord Jesus, I am fully convinced that no food is unclean in itself. But if anyone regards something as unclean, then for him it is unclean. If your brother is distressed because of what you eat, you are no longer acting in love. Do not by your eating destroy your brother for whom Christ died" (Romans 14:13-15 NIV).

This text may be applied to any religious view that is not a matter of salvation. It is a matter of meditation when Paul says to "make up your mind not to put any...obstacle in your brother's way" (Rom. 14:13 NIV). If done properly, this stage of meditation will reduce the negative elements our minds have built to protect our personal views. We are not trying to empty our minds of every belief we have until we believe in nothing. We are trying to open our minds to understand the various emotions and thoughts our minds have built as a protective barrier from the views of others.

Our minds are effective at building fortified walls that protect our views. The fact is that we define ourselves largely as an aggregate of our personal views. Many years have been invested in fortifying the things we have come to believe and trust in. Our mind uses all five functions, consciousness, memory, imagination, evaluation and estimation, to construct a fortified wall that serves as a protection for our stored views. The gate to enter or exit this wall is closely guarded by our mind. If an idea meets the standards of our mind's evaluation, it is allowed entry. If it contradicts our mind's scrutiny, it is rejected and even more fortifications are built up against it. The problem is that we often reject or accept the person tied to the view in the same way. We tend to associate only with those of similar opinions. We are averse to going to a place of worship not in our tradition. We do not listen to or read the teachings of those of another tradition. Our minds have established immediate responses that are raised when confronted with differing views and the people that hold them.

Paul addressed this problem in the Roman church. Defensive walls were dividing the people along the lines of their personal views. Paul did not assume that divisions were just the logical result of Christian faith and leave these divisions to result in demonimations and sects. Instead, he saw entrenched personal views as a harmful and took steps to help the Roman Christians to eliminate the barriers that these views caused. Our views are not as important as we think. In fact, they are harmful if we continue to fortify our views and exclude others whose views are different from ours. Paul directs the Roman Christians to think in a way that stops the promotion of division based on views. He encourages the strong in the faith to "give in" to the views of others (Rom. 14:13).

This exercise in truth encounter will lessen the tendency to judge others and harbor negative feelings because of their personal views. Our improper motivations build barriers of exclusion and ill feelings, but these may be diminished with the transforming power of the Holy Spirit. Through the meditation process, we will be more tolerant and accepting as we become aware of the mental fortress we have built in our own minds to keep others out and protect our own ideas. This is a worthy goal for us to aspire to. This is also the goal of the Holy Spirit. We cooperate with Him when we follow the admonition of Paul, "Let us therefore make every effort to do what leads to peace and to mutual edification" (Rom. 14:19 NIV).

Truth encounter is not an opportunity for you to become more convinced of the fact that you are right about everything. Becoming more convinced of personal views really accomplishes just the opposite of what we want. Through meditation we come to respect the various views held by others. We become aware of the walls of logic we have built to isolate ourselves from other views. This awareness leads to a dissatisfaction of living behind walls. We then begin the process of lowering our logical defenses. We begin to welcome thoughts that challenge our views. Those we considered our "opponents in the faith" we can truly respect, and even come to like. This is part of the process of the transformation of our mind. It takes a mature person to welcome challenges to what they have always believed. But this is the value of truth encounter.

Remember, faith is the motivation that the Holy Spirit is trying to instill as the most powerful motivation in our minds. Faith in Romans 14 does not result from a strict adherence to our own personal views to the exclusion of others. That is the definition of a weak faith according to Paul. Strong faith in this context is a deliberate awareness of the views of others and the determination not to cause tension or division because of differences in views. Faith is the ability to break out of our personal fortified views and welcome another on their terms without judgments arising in our minds. This is what we want the Holy Spirit to accomplish through meditation. We must do more than tolerate those of differing personal views. We must identify the judgments against them and eliminate them with the help of the Holy Spirit. This is a goal we can spend a lifetime trying to achieve. But through the transforming power of the Holy Spirit, our minds can interact in a way that fosters acceptance and unity even in the face of different views.

As this portion of your meditation concludes, evaluate the thoughts you are aware of and try to define the single ultimate truth the Holy Spirit is using to transform your mind. After some time in meditation, you will notice trends and a number of repeated truths that come to your mind again and again. Some examples of this kind of ultimate truth are the unity of the people of God, the sovereignty of God, the power of faith, the necessity of forgiveness, the holiness of God—the possible list is long. When you allow this one major truth to become prominent in your conscious mind you have accomplished a great deal. This is the summit of your meditation experience. This one ultimate truth is the gem that we have been mining for. We have prepared our mind to receive, cleared our mind of distractions and barriers and let the Holy Spirit speak. This one truth might remain at the front of your mind for several days or even weeks as you meditate. Do not think that each time you meditate you need to arrive at a unique summit truth. Allow the Holy Spirit to raise the truth He desires. Embrace that truth with your mind and welcome it as a transforming event.

Three meditation killers need to be identified and avoided: Study, thinking you know the topic well enough and expecting a unique revelation experience. We need to create a clean slate on which the Holy Spirit can impress His truth. A large part of being transformed is allowing our own personal views to diminish in their importance. A strong faith demands we prioritize and achieve peace with others. This requires a correct understanding of how our own views alienate us from others and create obstacles for peace. The goal of this truth encounter is to be transformed so that we do not pass judgment on others based on different perceptions of truth.

CHAPTER 8

STEPS 5-7: CONSECRATED FOR THE FUTURE

But you are a chosen race, a royal priesthood, a dedicated nation, [God's] own purchased, special people, that you may set forth the wonderful deeds and display the virtues and perfections of Him Who called you out of darkness into His marvelous light.

1 Peter 2:9, AMP

Step 5: God Awareness.

In step three we developed an awareness of God to help us deal with sins we remembered doing in the past. Through repentance and forgiveness we were prepared to encounter the truth of God. Now, after having yielding our mind to the Holy Spirit we have come to be aware of His truth (step 4). In this current step, we will develop an awareness of God that will assist us in directing our future actions and thoughts. We will refer to this state as "spirituality." The International Standard Bible Encyclopedia states that spirituality "signifies the state of a soul vitalized by the Divine Spirit and made alive unto God. It covers the entire range of man's faculties: intellect, feelings, will—all the attributes of personality." As we meditate on being a better spiritual person, we need a new sensitivity to come to our faculties.

New Vision. We must become aware that God is changing the way we perceive the world. God is wanting to increase the effectiveness of our vision. He is giving us eyes of faith so we see beyond the mere optical reality. Jesus said, "blessed are the pure in heart, for they shall see God" (Matt. 5:8). We are familiar with the term "eyes of faith." This describes an ability to perceive beyond what is seen with the natural eyes to what is seen by God. Early on the disciples often failed to see with faith. Jesus criticized them for having eyes but still not seeing and ears but still not hearing (Mk. 8:18). In contrast, the patriarchs of Hebrews 11 all had eyes of faith; "They did not receive the things promised; they only saw them and welcomed them from a distance" (Heb. 11:13). This kind of vision does not make problems disappear. It is not a pair of rose-colored glasses that throw a soft pink hue on the world's starkness. It is a new perspective that lifts our sight from underneath to view things from God's vantage point.

The psalmist asked God to "Open my eyes that I may see wonderful things in your law" (Ps. 119:18). This is not referring to natural vision. The eyes of the mind can be given vision to see into the invisible realm of God's work. Paul prays for this vision to be given to the Ephesian Christians. God gives new vision by making "your eyes focused and clear, so that you can see exactly what it is he is calling you to do, grasp the immensity of this glorious way of life he has for Christians, oh, the utter extravagance of his work in us who trust him — endless energy, boundless strength!" (Eph. 1:18, THE MESSAGE).

We do not need new horizons, we need new vision. We do not need new circumstances, we need new perspective. Our problems and failures are not beyond God's power to make right. We need to see the problems in life through the perspective of God. This is spiritual vision.

New Hearing. Spiritual hearing requires discernment. The voice of God is often quiet compared to the raging noise of the natural world. We tune our ears to hear sounds that we want to hear. If you were standing on a busy street of one of the larger cities of the world such as Calcutta, India, your ears would be assaulted with many different noises. You would hear horns, engines, and voices by the thousands within a few yards. But even in the middle of all of this noise, if you were to drop a handful of coins on the cement sidewalk, the subtle noise of the coins would arrest the ears of many people. They would immediately respond and come running in hopes of nabbing a few rupees. Doctors are trained to listen to your heartbeat and your breathing. What sounds like simple "noise" to the untrained ear is discerned with a great deal of understanding to a trained doctor. Auto mechanics are likewise able to listen to the mundane hum of an engine and determine what might be wrong simply by the sound. Hearing the voice of God is like that. Even in the noise of the activities of the day we can be in tune to hear the voice of the Holy Spirit. We do not need to be in mediation to hear God. We need to be familiar with what His voice sounds like. The common phrase Jesus used was, "whoever has ears, let him hear."

We might assume that God seldom speaks to us. I believe that assumption to be largely wrong. John's Gospel records the teaching of Jesus about the coming of the Spirit and the role He is to play in the lives of the Christian believers. The Spirit will "bring to remembrance all that I said unto you." In 15:26 the communication of the Spirit will testify of Jesus. Again in 16:14, "He shall glorify me: for he shall take of mine, and shall declare it unto you." One of the main functions of the Spirit is to teach, declare, remind and testify to Christians. The mind of the individual Christian is the sphere of the

Spirit's speaking. It is within the mind that we must develop "ears to hear."

New Thinking. The spiritual mind can think the thoughts of God. Paul explains in 1 Cor. 2:11-16 that the Holy Spirit can discern and comprehend every thought in the mind of God—thoughts about the future in heaven, thoughts about activities here on earth, thoughts towards individuals—there is nothing in the mind of God that is kept secret from the Holy Spirit. In fact, the Holy Spirit deliberately "searches all things, even the deep things of God (1 Cor. 2:10). The Spirit does not keep this knowledge a secret. In fact, the Spirit of God continually operates on the mind of the Christian, bringing adjustments to our reasoning and clarity to our ability to think the thoughts as God would think them. We are constantly reminded in subtle ways of the will of God and nudged toward fulfilling His purposes in our daily journey of faith. God's presence is continually present in order that we may know and act according to the "mind of Christ" in every situation we will face. As we allow new ways of thinking we will also be better able to evaluate ideas that arise in our minds and determine whether or not they are spiritually beneficial. If not, we can "demolish" that concept and make it "obedient" to the mind of Christ (2 Cor. 10:5).

These three faculties, vision, hearing and thinking are directly affected by the presence of God in our lives. We must cultivate an ongoing awareness of God that helps us realize that our sight is one of faith, our ears are always in tune to hear His voice and our minds are uncluttered, disciplined and in tune with His thoughts.

In order to develop a God-awareness for the future, we must be able to predict the kind of situations we will encounter in the day ahead of us. Visualize yourself at work, at school or in a difficult situation with another person. See also that God's presence is right there with you. Determine that you will use His vision, hear His voice and think His thoughts no matter how difficult things become. This determination to act based on God's vision, hearing and thinking is called consecration. Consecration has many shades of meaning in the Bible. It means to be dedicated, to be holy, to make new, to set apart, to be ordained. The admonition of Paul is for the Corinthians to consecrate themselves: "I urge you, brothers, in view of God's mercy, to offer your bodies as living sacrifices, holy and pleasing to God" (Rom. 12:1). This is only possible after there has been a transforming of the mind by the power of the Holy Spirit (v. 13). Visualize your emotions and will coming into agreement with the thoughts of God. The Holy Spirit inside of you is determined to please God. Let that determination become the influence that will guide you through the activities and circumstances of the day.

Step 6: Mind Awareness.

In step 2 we became aware of the thoughts our mind entertained in the past. In this step, however, we will develop an awareness of how our minds are being changed to conform to the mind of Christ. As we have stated, it is possible for our mind to think the thoughts of God. This requires a judgment of ideas that arise in our mind. Paul mentions that we "demolish arguments and every pretension that sets itself up against the knowledge of God, and we take captive every thought to make it obedient to Christ (2 Cor. 10:5). The method for this violent mental action is to use weapons of the Spirit (v. 4). The picture Paul presents is a military illustration. Once a thought is identified as harmful to our spirituality, we literally subdue it (tear it down, cast it down) and lead it as a prisoner of war into the fortified stronghold controlled by Christ. It is unreasonable to assume that Paul is suggesting that we stop every thought as it occurs and evaluate it. Since thoughts arise in such rapid succession, this would be impossible. Instead, Paul sees his mind as a fortified stronghold in which Christ exercises supreme authority through the Holy Spirit. Every thought is made to proceed through this fortification. Any thought that is impure is destroyed absolutely with the weapons of the Spirit. These weapons are mighty and effective for the destruction of any thought that is opposed to the mind of Christ. Only the thoughts that are in agreement with the Spirit are allowed to take root in our consciousness. The key for us is to establish a mind that is completely fortified with the presence of the Holy Spirit. We must give the Holy Spirit the authority to destroy thoughts that contradict the thoughts of God. This process is established as we develop a mind-awareness and assist in the process of leading thoughts as prisoners to the place of the Spirit's authority and power.

We can protect any thought from being destroyed by the Spirit. We can build areas in our mind in which the Spirit has no authority to destroy. It is in these places that we harbor treasonous thoughts. We allow lust, bitterness an ungodly ideas to dwell safely, beyond the reach of the Spirit's weapons. These places Paul calls "strongholds" and they are in contention with the Spirit to control our mind and motivate our actions. We must become intimately aware of our own mind and willingly submit these places of refuge for unspiritual thoughts to the cleansing power of the Holy Spirit. This is a freeing influence on our minds. Strongholds seek to direct our thinking away from the possibilities of faith. Influenced by lust and greed we think of pleasing primarily ourselves. Influenced by anger and bitterness we think of hurting others. When we destroy these strongholds we free our minds to break the limits our strongholds have set.

Even today we would consider the Apostle Paul a daring and progressive thinker. His ideas were often outside the standard of what was considered "orthodox". Yet God used the mind of Paul to express the Gospel in unique ways. His logic and defense of the Gospel was pure and his thoughts seldom misdirected. Perhaps the reason is that Paul practiced what he preached. His willingness to subject every thought to the Spirit led to the destroying of strongholds that commonly existed in his day. One example is the idea of preaching the message of Christ to the Gentiles. Even the other Apostles struggled with this idea. Through a process, Paul's mind was free to think and dream according to the mind of Christ. This is a worthy goal: to know our mind and to submit our strongholds to the power of God. To do so is to free our mind to think the thoughts of God and accomplish his purposes.

As you become aware of how your mind operates, you will begin to notice areas that do not conform to the mind of Christ. If thoughts of doubt, fear, unforgiveness, lust, anger, self-pity, depression and the like occur on a regular basis, or are tied to specific people or circumstances, we must allow God to break these strongholds and lead these thoughts as prisoners into His realm of power and control. This is not a process we can do once and call it finished. This is a lifestyle that must continue on order to keep our minds in tune with the mind of

Christ. Use this time of meditation to honestly become aware of the strongholds built in your own mind and allow God's power to transform that area with His power.

Step 7: Body Awareness.

In step 1 we recalled the actions done in the past that were displeasing to God. In this step we will consider how our actions in the future can be used to glorify God. First we must determine not to offer our body to participate in sinful acts. We are creatures of habit. Sins committed in the past have a strong hold on us. We must deliberately choose to avoid recommitting these sins. Consider the following passage:

"It is God's will that you should be sanctified: that you should avoid sexual immorality; that each of you should learn to control his own body in a way that is holy and honorable, not in passionate lust like the heathen, who do not know God; and that in this matter no one should wrong his brother or take advantage of him. The Lord will punish men for all such sins, as we have already told you and warned you. For God did not call us to be impure, but to live a holy life" (1 Thess 4:3-7).

"Control" is a word that demands our attention. We must be more deliberate at controlling our bodies. When we control something, we set boundaries for it and keep it within limits we have set. Control presumes discipline and obedience. The same must be true of our bodies. There are several simple strategies you can use to control your body and enable it to be an instrument of righteousness.

Guard your senses. Be aware of what you are looking at, hearing, and putting into your body. Don't let your senses just run at will. Keep your eyes, ears, tongue and body in a state of constant supervision. We cannot always control what image passes before our eyes, but we can control how long our gaze stays fixed there. The first look is free, but the second look is often a lack of controlling our eyes. Use things for their function rather than status. The clothes we wear and the car we drive should not be chosen based how much status they bring us. Our bodies have very little to do with our character. It is not what is outside that determines anything of significance in God's eyes. Reputation is shallow and may be a facade of material and gadgets. Our true identity is revealed when our "stuff" is removed from us. It is a good exercise to become mindful of how you use clothes, jewelry, food, shelter and other possessions. Desire for status often impedes our ability to be instruments of righteousness.

Endure uncomfortable situations without complaining. If the restaurant is too hot and the food is too cold try making yourself enjoy your meal without having to complain to the waitress. Let the driver behind you go around you instead of intentionally keeping ahead to irritate him. Too often we overemphasize our personal comfort. Thoughts like "That's not what I ordered!" and "He can just drive the speed limit like the rest of us!" are in need of evaluation. The emotions that accompany such thoughts are seldom spiritually beneficial. No wonder we are unwilling to take time and money to help a stranger or witness to an unsaved acquaintance since we do not have and discipline to endure uncomfortable circumstances. In time we can learn that what we once considered unpleasant and highly irritating can be endured with little or no difficulty. Eventually we may even come to value the waitress and the other driver as more important than our personal comfort.

Avoid compromising people, objects and situations. If you consistently give in to bad deeds because of your association with specific people, stop spending extended time with them. Remove things that promote your inability to please God with your body. Avoid situations where doing the wrong thing is easy. One of the parts of our body that needs constant supervision is our tongue. Few things land us in hot water as effectively as our words. The problem is, once we say something, we cannot just recall the words. As soon as they are spoken the damage is done. So, it is beneficial for us to screen our words before we speak. Develop a discipline of not speaking your mind. After all, people who "just say what's on their mind" are the most miserable people I know. They suffer tremendously because of what they say. Determine stop harmful words before they form on your tongue. "Do not let any unwholesome talk come out of your mouths, but only what is helpful for building others up according to their needs, that it may benefit those who listen" (Eph. 4:29). It is very liberating to sit in meditation at the end of the day and not be sorry for criticisms and poor choices of words committed during the day. It may seem painful to hold your tongue in the heat of the moment, but think ahead to the remorse you will feel when the Holy Spirit brings the episode to your mind as you meditate. It is possible to go one whole day without complaining verbally. In fact, Paul suggests that we can live a lifestyle in which we do not complain or argue at all. His admonition to the Philippians was to "do everything without complaining or arguing, so that you may become blameless and pure, children of God without fault in a crooked and depraved generation, in which you shine like stars in the universe as you hold out the word of life" (Phil. 2:14-16). When we complain and criticize we say more about ourselves than we do someone else. It is a beneficial discipline to develop an ability to arrest unwholesome words. It indicates that we have control over our bodies. "We all stumble in many ways. If anyone is never at fault in what he says, he is a perfect man, able to keep his whole body in check" (James 3:2).

Body awareness prepares us to serve God in difficult situations with difficult people. If we can overlook our own discomfort, we are better able to realize the benefit we can provide others. This includes being generous at our own expense. As Jesus teaches:

"Do not resist an evil person. If someone strikes you on the right cheek, turn to him the other also. And if someone wants to sue you and take your tunic, let him have your cloak as well. 41 If someone forces you to go one mile, go with him two miles. Give to the one who asks you, and do not turn away from the one who wants to borrow from you" (Matt. 5:39-42).

Our bodies are instruments that can be used for God's purposes if we are mindful to avoid prioritizing our own needs and wants above those of others. "Do nothing out of selfish ambition or vain conceit, but in humility consider others better than yourselves. Each of you should look not only to your own interests, but also to the interests of others (Phil. 2:3-4).

In addition to generosity, we must develop body awareness so that we can endure suffering for Christ. When Paul reminded Timothy of the many sufferings he endured in various places he traveled, he said in no uncertain terms that not only he, but "In fact, everyone who wants to live a godly life in Christ Jesus will be persecuted" (2 Tim 3:12). Enduring personal pain is something no Christian can justly avoid. When we act in obedience to the Holy Spirit we "shine like stars", "are the salt of the earth, "are a city set on a hill". There is no hiding. If our friends and co-workers do not know we are a Christian, we are not acting in obedience to the mind of Christ. So, we must use this time in meditation to determine that we will "create" a little persecution for ourselves. Visualize yourself sharing the gospel with a friend. See yourself offering to pray for someone struggling with health issues. See yourself saying "no" to compromising activities even if it causes you some ridicule. The words of Paul here are probably too far above any of us to fully comprehend, but they serve to remind us of our duty to endure hardships. "I eagerly expect and hope that I will in no way be ashamed, but will have sufficient courage so that now as always Christ will be exalted in my body , whether by life or by death. For to me, to live is Christ and to die is gain" (Phil. 1:20-21). Now, what was that reason you had for not witnessing to your friend?

The last three steps of our meditation prepare us for future action. God-awareness invites the Holy Spirit to bring transformation to our minds in a way that we see things from God's perspective. It fine-tunes our hearing to discern God's voice. It also directs our minds to be able to think the thoughts of God. Through mind-awareness we recognize our own personal mental strongholds and allow the Spirit to tear down those ideas in order to make them conform to the mind of Christ. Finally, body-awareness prepares us to act in a holy manner; being generous and recognizing opportunities to be a blessing to others. Body awareness will also prepare us to endure suffering as a result of our obedience to Christ.

CHAPTER 9

TRANSITIONING FROM MEDITATION

An empty-head thinks mischief is fun,
but a mindful person relishes wisdom.
--Proverbs 10:23, The Message

At this point you have completed your session of meditation. Take a moment and say a prayer sealing the accomplishments of your meditation. Don't be in a hurry to leave the state of mindfulness you have created for yourself. Mindfulness is more than an occasional practice during meditation. "We ought to assist the weak, being mindful of the words of the Lord Jesus, how He Himself said, It is more blessed (makes one happier and more to be envied) to give than to receive (Acts 20:35 AMP). We are to keep aware of the opportunities that present themselves during the day. Specifically, "as occasion and opportunity open up to us, let us do good [morally] to all people [not only being useful or profitable to them, but also doing what is for their spiritual good and advantage]. Be mindful to be a blessing, especially to those of the household of faith [those who belong to God's family with you, the believers]" (Gal. 6:10 AMP). This mindfulness searches the times and seizes the opportunities to be a blessing. So many chances pass us by because we simply have not developed an awareness to do good at every opportunity. Now after meditating your awareness has turned toward the Holy Spirit who has in turn directed you to perceive the world and everyone in it in a new way. No longer are others a troublesome inconvenience to your wishes. They have become your purpose and object of your awareness. This is so because those same people are the focus of the Lord's awareness.

"The LORD has been mindful of us;

He will bless us;

He will bless the house of Israel;

He will bless the house of Aaron.

He will bless those who fear the LORD,

Both small and great" (Ps. 115:12-13 NKJV).

You may want to keep a journal of your meditative journey. If you already keep a prayer journal or journal your day's activities it is easy to add a section to record your thoughts after meditation. If is important to wait until after you have finished, however. Reading or writing interfere with the focused thoughts meditation tries to achieve. You will no doubt come to be quite ready to spend regular time meditation. It is an exercise in which we can become transformed in mind and refreshed in body. If you currently schedule time for a nap or quiet time, try to incorporate a time of meditation in place of sleep or simple rest. 15 minutes is enough time to focus the mind. Although 40 minutes to an hour is a more reasonable time period to get through the seven steps adequately.

Meditation has been long neglected by our Christian tradition. My hope is that you will be some of the first to recapture the benefits of this discipline. My additional hope is that more people will begin to write and prepare further aids and explanations of Christian meditation techniques. As your mind prospers my sincere prayer is that your life will be richer and more full of the presence of God. We all have much work to do to fully embrace the mind of our Savior, Jesus Christ. But the Bible is full of hope for us that we are indeed being renewed day by day. Our minds are undergoing the transforming work of the Holy Spirit. This process can be assisted by our efforts. May we all seek to increase the rate at which we are becoming like our blessed Savior.

APPENDIX 1

Quick Guide to Transformation Meditation

1. Body Awareness.

Focus on breathing and body functions. Be mindful of your memories arising of past actions of your body. Remember any actions that need to be forgiven.

2. Mind Awareness.

Focus on feelings and emotions. Be mindful of your recent thought patterns. Remember any thoughts or patterns that need to be forgiven.

3. God Awareness.

Focus on the presence of God to forgive and restore. Visualize your purity as you silently confess the sins that have arisen in your mind.

4. Truth Encounter.

Focus on a single aspect of God's truth. Use one of the helps in the book if needed. Be aware of your own theories and allow the Holy Spirit to develop a proper perspective in you towards the views of others. Review the Meditation Killers if needed.

5. God Awareness.

Focus on the presence of God and the things He wants to change in your mind. In order to live a holy life we need further transformation of our vision, hearing and thinking.

6. Mind Awareness.

Focus on the contents of your mind. Recognize patterns and strongholds that need to be destroyed. Visualize yourself thinking in perfect agreement with the mind of Christ.

7.   Body Awareness.

Focus on the ways you will exercise control over your body actions. Determine to guard your senses and words carefully. Think of staying mindful of opportunities to be a blessing. Prepare your mind to endure some level of suffering for the cause of Jesus Christ.

APPENDIX 2

Meditation Killers

Study.

During meditation is not the time to search your Bible encyclopedia for background information. No matter how strong the urge to look up information, don't do it. Keep your mind focused on the subject at hand without giving in to the urge to expand your knowledge of the subject. The goal of meditation is not to learn new knowledge, but to become more keenly aware of what you already know.

"I already know the subject thoroughly enough."

There is benefit in meditating on God's grace, or the nature of the incarnation, or the value of the human soul even if you consider yourself an expert on the subject. There are facets of truth that lay hidden from us until we take the time to contemplate them in just the right way over a period of time.

Expecting a "revelation" of new, unique truth.

The best scriptural meditation subjects are commonly known and simple truths—God's law, the past miracles of God and the promises of God. As exciting as a new and unique revelation is, the priority remains that "we must be sure to obey the truth we have learned already" (Phil. 3:16 NLT).

APPENDIX 3

Sample Meditations

The following pages contain some sample meditations. Each of the steps of meditation are noted. Make sure you do not simply jump to the Scripture verse, read it and then go on with your day. Deliberately take a moment to advance through each step. We are intentionally preparing to listen, listening, then mentally applying what we hear in preparation for daily activities.

MEDITATION 1

1.   Body Awareness
2.   Mind Awareness
3.   God Awareness
4.   Truth Encounter

We know that all things work together for the good of those who love God—those whom he has called according to his plan.

Romans 12:2 GOD'S WORD
Translation

5.   God Awareness
6.   Mind Awareness
7.   Body Awareness

MEDITATION 2

1.   Body Awareness
2.   Mind Awareness
3.   God Awareness
4.   Truth Encounter

This is how you should pray:
Our Father in heaven,
  let your name be kept holy.
   Let your kingdom come.
  Let your will be done on earth
    as it is done in heaven.
  Give us our daily bread today.
   Forgive us as we forgive others.
   Don't allow us to be tempted.
  Instead, rescue us from the evil one
                    Matthew 6:9-13 GOD'S WORD
                                  Translation

5.   God Awareness
6.   Mind Awareness
7.   Body Awareness

MEDITATION 3

1.   Body Awareness
2.   Mind Awareness
3.   God Awareness
4.   Truth Encounter

We know that all things work together for the good of those who love God—those whom he has called according to his plan.

> Romans 8:28 GOD'S WORD
> Translation

5.   God Awareness
6.   Mind Awareness
7.   Body Awareness

MEDITATION 4

1.   Body Awareness
2.   Mind Awareness
3.   God Awareness
4.   Truth Encounter

Create a clean heart in me, O God,
    and renew a faithful spirit within me.
Do not force me away from your presence,
    and do not take your Holy Spirit from me.
Restore the joy of your salvation to me,
    and provide me with a spirit of willing obedience
                    Psalm 51:10-13 GOD'S WORD
                                Translation

5.   God Awareness
6.   Mind Awareness
7.   Body Awareness

U of A Emergency Social Committee
Proudly Presents

WINE SURVIVOR

$10 per entry + $20 bottle of wine
Improve your chances with immunities
$5 / immunity to a maximum of 3

No. 010

MEDITATION 5

1.   Body Awareness
2.   Mind Awareness
3.   God Awareness
4.   Truth Encounter

But the spiritual nature produces love, joy, peace, patience, kindness, goodness, faithfulness, gentleness, and self-control. There are no laws against things like that.

Galatians 5:22-23 GOD'S WORD
Translation

5.   God Awareness
6.   *Mind* Awareness
7.   Body *A*wareness

MEDITATION 6

1.   Body Awareness
2.   Mind Awareness
3.   God Awareness
4.   Truth Encounter

Yet, the strength of those who wait with hope in the LORD
   will be renewed.
      They will soar on wings like eagles.
      They will run and won't become weary.
      They will walk and won't grow tired.
              Isaiah 40:31 GOD'S WORD
                    Translation

5.   God Awareness
6.   Mind Awareness
7.   Body Awareness

MEDITATION 7

1.   Body Awareness
2.   Mind Awareness
3.   God Awareness
4.   Truth Encounter

But (Jesus) told me: "My kindness[a] is all you need. My power is strongest when you are weak." So I will brag even more about my weaknesses in order that Christ's power will live in me.

2 Corinthians 12:9 GOD'S WORD
Translation

5.   God Awareness
6.   Mind Awareness
7.   Body Awareness

MEDITATION 8

1.   Body Awareness
2. Mind Awareness
3. God Awareness
4. Truth Encounter

Jesus said, "I can guarantee this truth: Those who listen to what I say and believe in the one who sent me will have eternal life. They won't be judged because they have already passed from death to life."

John 5:24 GOD'S WORD
Translation

5. God Awareness
6. Mind Awareness
7. Body Awareness

MEDITATION 9

1. Body Awareness
2. Mind Awareness
3. God Awareness
4. Truth Encounter

Trust the LORD with all your heart,
and do not rely on your own understanding.
In all your ways acknowledge him,
and he will make your paths smooth.

Proverbs 3:5-6 GOD'S WORD
Translation

5. God Awareness
6. Mind Awareness
7. Body Awareness

MEDITATION 10

1.   Body Awareness
2.   Mind Awareness
3.   God Awareness
4.   Truth Encounter

I know the plans that I have for you, declares the LORD. They are plans for peace and not disaster, plans to give you a future filled with hope.

Jeremiah 29:11 GOD'S WORD
Translation

5.   God Awareness
6.   Mind Awareness
7.   Body Awareness

Printed in Great Britain
by Amazon